Building Your Home Through Effective Role-Play

Transform Your Family Dynamics Today Through Effective Role

Management Techniques for a Successful Relationship

Adegboye S. Aduragbemi

INTRODUCTION

In addition to being a relationship based on love, trust, and shared objectives, marriage is also characterized by the assignment of roles and responsibilities. Navigating the many duties and tasks within a marriage, from money management to housework, frequently creates concerns about mutual support, communication, and expectations. "Roles and Responsibilities FAQ in Marriage" is a helpful resource for married couples who are looking for direction, comprehension, and hands-on assistance in identifying and carrying out their responsibilities in the partnership.

This book contains a thorough list of frequently asked questions, thoughtful responses, and professional guidance specific to the subtleties of roles and responsibilities in marriage. Most of the queries, either conventional or contemporary, are answered with compassion, comprehension, and practical advice to assist couples in resolving the difficulties of their shared obligations with grace and purpose.

"Roles and Responsibilities FAQ in Marriage" gives couples a road map for promoting cooperation, establishing mutual respect, and fortifying their marriage with relevant tales, real-life situations, and evidence-based tactics. This book offers priceless insights and valuable tools to help you, whether you're a newlywed figuring out the division of labor or an experienced couple looking to realign your roles and negotiate the complexity of duties and responsibilities with resilience and confidence.

May you find comfort in other people's experiences that you have shared, inspiration in the knowledge of professionals, and the bravery to accept your duties and responsibilities as a means of achieving a deeper level of fulfillment and connection in your marriage as you set out on this path of research and discovery.

Together, let's explore the ageless issues, complex details, and allure of roles and obligations in marriage.

Chapter One

Your duty is needed in building your relationship.

Illustration of a destroyed relationship

Mia and Jason used to be the definition of a power couple in the vibrant metropolis of Metroville. They dreamed of creating a successful and happy life together when they first met in college, fell in love, and started dating. But, as they dealt with the difficulties of adulthood, their relationship began to fall apart due to competing roles and obligations.

As a gifted marketing executive, Mia was highly driven and committed to her work. She loved the fast-paced atmosphere of the business world and was always looking for ways to do better and be recognized. Jason, a kind educator who is passionate about teaching, committed himself to his students and the challenges of his line of work in the meantime.

Mia and Jason's relationship was tense and resentful due to their different priorities and obligations, despite their mutual love and dedication to one another. To further her profession,

6

Mia frequently found herself working on the weekends and late into the night, missing out on valuable time with Jason. Jason, meanwhile, yearned for Mia's understanding and support in his pursuits and felt abandoned and undervalued.

As the years went by, resentment and discontentment clouded Mia and Jason's once-loving partnership, causing their relationship to grow more tense. The attempts to reach a compromise and find a solution to their problems all failed despite their best efforts to express their wants and worries to one another. Mia became resentful of what she saw as Jason's lack of ambition, while Jason thought Mia's unwavering will to succeed at whatever cost was stifling.

Their respective roles and responsibilities turned into a point of dispute, causing a rift and weakening the basis of their partnership. They were unable to come to an agreement or compromise and quarreled nonstop over money, careers, and who should do what around the house. Their once-loving relationship turned into a never-ending loop of discontent, hatred, and finger-pointing.

Ultimately, realizing their duties and responsibilities had irreversibly destroyed their relationship, Mia and Jason made the painful decision to split up. They both blamed the other for their relationship's breakdown as they lamented the loss of their former love.

Years later, Mia and Jason coincidentally crossed paths once more. They couldn't help but feel a twinge of grief for the love they had lost as they made small talk. They realized that their roles and obligations had wrecked their relationship, and they wished they had placed a higher priority on mutual support, communication, and understanding.

This story shows how competing duties and obligations may strain even the most solid relationships, emphasizing the value of open communication and willingness to make concessions and support one another in building strong, long-lasting bonds.

Illustration of a building relationship

Sophia and Adam were two people in the busy metropolis of Metroville with different lives and duties, but whose paths crossed to create a solid and lasting friendship. Adam, a committed teacher with a love of learning, and Sophia, a social worker committed to serving others, got to know each other through a community outreach program.

While they were polite and professional in their early exchanges, as they collaborated, they found a shared dedication to improving their town. Adam was motivated by Sophia's compassion and understanding for those in need, and Sophia appreciated Adam's commitment to his students.

Their business partnership developed into a close friendship and, ultimately, a love one over time. They shared their hopes, anxieties, and plans for the future while finding comfort and happiness in one other's company.

As their bond grew, Sophia and Adam saw how much their duties and responsibilities complemented one another and contributed to their compatibility. Adam's ability to be organized completed Sophia's creative energy, and Sophia's maternal personality complemented Adam's supporting approach. They forged a solid alliance based on respect, understanding, and common objectives.

As they overcame obstacles and shared life's delights, their duties and responsibilities formed the cornerstone of their relationship. Whether they were working together on community projects or helping one other through challenging times at work, Sophia and Adam found strength and meaning in their connection.

As their love deepened, Sophia and Adam made a promise to one another and exchanged vows in front of loved ones in a touching ceremony. They accepted their duties and responsibilities as partners because they knew that by working together, they could get over any challenges and realize their goals.

Years later, Sophia and Adam reflected gratefully and warmly on their adventure. They came to see that a solid foundation of mutual support, shared values, and a thorough awareness of each other's roles and responsibilities had formed the basis of their partnership.

They realized that their relationship would only get stronger with time, and because they accepted each other's unique qualities and worked as a team, their love blossomed.

This story highlights the value of cooperation, understanding, and mutual support in developing a solid and long-lasting connection by showing how a relationship may be established based on shared roles and responsibilities.

Chapter Two

Striking balance in marriage

In our marriage, how do we establish and discuss roles and responsibilities?

Clear communication, respect for one another, and a readiness to make concessions are necessary for defining and negotiating roles and duties. To begin, talk about the expectations, preferences, and strengths of each spouse concerning childcare, finances, domestic chores, and other obligations. Be adaptable and ready to change course as necessary to take into account new demands and situations.

How can we deal with traditional expectations of roles and obligations in our marriage and gender stereotypes?

Challenging social norms, accepting equality, and sharing responsibilities inside the marriage are necessary steps toward addressing gender stereotypes and traditional expectations. Talk openly about the potential effects of gender roles on your relationship and how to divide up work and duties according to personal availability, interests, and talents rather than following conventional gender roles.

What should we do if one spouse feels overburdened or bitter about their position in the marriage?

It's critical to deal with a partner's feelings of overload or resentment regarding their role or obligations in the marriage proactively and positively. Encourage honest discussion of emotions and worries, then collaborate to identify solutions that lighten the load and advance a more equitable distribution of duties. To lessen the workload and lessen stress, think about outsourcing duties or, if needed, enlisting outside assistance.

How can we resolve disputes or arguments about roles and obligations in our marriage?

Finding common ground, being willing to compromise, and using good communication is necessary when handling conflicts or disagreements on duties and responsibilities. Actively listen to each other's viewpoints, show compassion and understanding, and collaborate to find solutions that satisfy the requirements and preferences of both parties. Concentrate on coming up with win-win ideas that encourage cooperation and harmony in the marriage.

How can we make sure that each spouse feels that their contributions to the marriage are recognized and appreciated?

Regularly express thanks and acknowledgment for each other's contributions to make sure both partners feel important and appreciated. Celebrate and acknowledge each other's accomplishments and efforts, and express gratitude for the various ways that each partner contributes to the success and general well-being of the marriage.

In our marriage, how do we establish and discuss roles and responsibilities?

Clear communication, respect for one another, and a readiness to make concessions are necessary for defining and negotiating roles and duties. To begin, talk about the expectations, preferences, and strengths of each spouse concerning childcare, finances, domestic chores, and other obligations. Be adaptable and ready to change course as necessary to take into account new demands and situations.

What are some typical difficulties that couples run into when trying to divide up household duties and responsibilities?

Couples may have difficulties when it comes to allocating household chores and obligations, such as uneven labor distribution, divergent standards of neatness or organization, and disagreements over particular activities or duties. To overcome these obstacles, have honest conversations, establish reasonable expectations, and come up with solutions that benefit all parties equally.

What measures can we take to guarantee that each spouse feels free to express their wants and preferences for roles and duties in the marriage?

Fostering a communicative atmosphere that is encouraging and helpful is necessary to guarantee that both partners feel empowered to express their wants and preferences. Encourage an environment where respect and active listening are valued, and provide each partner with the chance to voice their ideas, emotions, and worries without worrying about criticism or condemnation. Recognize one another's viewpoints and work together to develop solutions that respect the needs and preferences of both parties.

How can we strike a balance between aggressiveness and compromise while determining duties and responsibilities in a marriage?

To negotiate duties and responsibilities within a marriage, compromise is necessary since it enables both parties to have their needs satisfied while still honoring the autonomy and preferences of the other. It is crucial to strike a balance between assertiveness and compromise by standing up for one's wants and boundaries while also being willing to offer and receive. Use aggressive communication strategies, such as using "I" statements and politely and directly expressing your wants, but also have an open mind to discovering points of agreement and win-win solutions.

How might cultural or societal expectations influence roles and obligations within a marriage, and how can we as a couple handle these influences?

Attitudes and actions about gender roles, domestic duties, and family dynamics can be significantly influenced by cultural or societal expectations, which can also have a substantial effect on roles and obligations inside a marriage. As a relationship, navigating these pressures means identifying and questioning conventional conventions and stereotypes that might not line up with your beliefs or tastes. Discuss cultural and societal expectations openly and honestly, and look into ways to build a partnership that aligns with your shared goals, values, and beliefs.

What should we do if one spouse feels overburdened or exhausted by their marital tasks and responsibilities?

It's critical to deal with a partner's feelings of overwhelm or burnout in a proactive and caring manner. Discuss the causes of their stress or tiredness in an open and sincere discussion, then collaborate to come up with workable fixes and support networks. If possible, think about splitting up duties or responsibilities, outsourcing some of the work, and looking into strategies to support each partner's wellness and self-care.

How may we resolve disputes or problems about duties and obligations in our marriage without jeopardizing intimacy or trust?

To resolve conflicts or disagreements about roles and responsibilities, polite conversation, attentive listening, and a desire to establish common ground are necessary. Rather than viewing arguments as dangers to your relationship, view them as chances for development and understanding. Prioritize preserving closeness, mutual respect, and trust in the marriage while concentrating on finding solutions that respect each partner's needs and preferences.

In our marriage, how can we cultivate a sense of reciprocal accountability and responsibility, particularly concerning common objectives and commitments?

Establishing a culture of reciprocal accountability and responsibility entails being transparent in communication, holding one another accountable for agreements made, and defining clear expectations. Establish a shared vision and objectives for your marriage, then check in frequently to evaluate how things are going and resolve any issues that may come up. Together, celebrate your successes and help one other get through any obstacles you may have encountered.

Chapter Three

Questions about some other crucial factors that affect

communication in marriage

Regarding assigning and receiving tasks and obligations in our marriage, how can we cultivate a spirit of cooperation and teamwork?

Encourage cooperation and teamwork by placing a high value on honest communication, support from one another, and a shared dedication to the marriage's success. View assignments and obligations as chances to collaborate with others to achieve shared objectives and recognize successes as a group. Establish a welcoming and inclusive atmosphere where both partners are empowered to contribute to the partnership and feel appreciated and respected.

What steps should we take if one spouse believes their contributions to the marriage are not appreciated or acknowledged?

It's critical to handle the situation with compassion and understanding if one partner believes that their contributions are not appreciated or acknowledged. It is essential to recognize and affirm their frustrations and dissatisfactions by listening to them without passing judgment. Collaborate to determine strategies for enhancing mutual respect, communication, and recognition of each other's contributions to the marriage.

Suppose one partner feels that their tasks are more significant or demanding than the other. How can we encourage equality and justice in the allocation of roles and responsibilities within our marriage?

Mutual respect, openness, and cooperation are necessary for promoting equality and justice in the distribution of tasks and duties. Instead of putting cultural standards or traditional gender roles to use when assigning values to specific activities or obligations, concentrate on forging a partnership in which each partner's contributions are appreciated and valued. Make sure the effort is distributed fairly by checking in with each other regularly. If there are any apparent imbalances, modify them as necessary.

In the framework of their duties and obligations in marriage, how can we make sure that both partners have opportunities for personal development, fulfillment, and self-care?

By placing a high priority on balance and welfare in the marriage, you can make sure that both spouses have possibilities for personal development, fulfillment, and self-care. In addition to supporting one another in finding time for self-care and relaxation, encourage one another to pursue interests, hobbies, and goals outside of their positions and duties. Establish a relationship that appreciates and promotes cooperation and mutual support in addition to personal development and satisfaction.

What are some typical difficulties that couples run into when trying to divide up household duties and responsibilities?

Couples may have difficulties when it comes to allocating household chores and obligations, such as uneven labor distribution, divergent standards of neatness or organization, and disagreements over particular activities or duties. To overcome these obstacles, have honest conversations, establish reasonable expectations, and come up with solutions that benefit all parties equally.

How can we resolve disputes or arguments about roles and obligations in our marriage?

Finding common ground, being willing to compromise, and using good communication is necessary when handling conflicts or disagreements about duties and responsibilities. Actively listen to each other's viewpoints, show compassion and understanding, and collaborate to find solutions that satisfy the requirements and preferences of both parties. Concentrate on coming up with win-win ideas that encourage cooperation and harmony in the marriage.

How can we make sure that each spouse feels that their contributions to the marriage are recognized and appreciated?

Regularly express thanks and acknowledgment for each other's contributions to make sure both partners feel important and appreciated. Celebrate and acknowledge each other's accomplishments and efforts, and express gratitude for the various ways that each partner contributes to the success and general well-being of the marriage.

What should we do if one spouse feels overburdened or bitter about their position in the marriage?

It's critical to deal with a partner's feelings of overload or resentment regarding their role or obligations in the marriage proactively and positively. Encourage honest discussion of emotions and worries, then collaborate to identify solutions that lighten the load and advance a more equitable distribution of duties. To lessen the workload and lessen stress, think about outsourcing duties or, if needed, enlisting outside assistance.

How important is flexibility in a marriage when it comes to assigning and receiving obligations, particularly when things change over time?

Managing duties and responsibilities in a marriage requires flexibility, particularly when circumstances change over time. Be open to making necessary adjustments to fit in with new difficulties, priorities, and life stages. Openly discuss any changes in wants or expectations, and work together to come up with original solutions that promote the pleasure and well-being of both parties.

How can we assign work successfully, and what part does delegation play in managing roles and obligations within a marriage?

Since delegation enables each spouse to capitalize on their unique skills and strengths, it is essential for effectively managing roles and duties within a marriage. Determine what can be assigned to each partner depending on their preferences, talents, and availability. Be explicit in your communication on deadlines and expectations. Have faith in one another to see through assigned duties and provide assistance and criticism as required to guarantee their completion.

In our marriage, how can we resolve discrepancies in standards or expectations for finishing assignments and carrying out obligations?

Empathy, compromise, and a dedication to identifying common ground are necessary when managing disparities in norms or expectations. Respect and acknowledge one another's viewpoints and make an effort to comprehend the logic underlying different standards or expectations. Collaborate to create agreements or standards that respect each partner's inclinations and foster collaboration and harmony in the marriage.

How can we make sure that the way we divide up the tasks and responsibilities encourages personal development for both of us?

Make sure that the tasks and obligations you assign each other support personal development and progress by motivating one another to pursue interests, objectives, and hobbies outside of your shared responsibilities. Establish learning, exploration, and self-improvement opportunities, and encourage one another to follow your dreams and ambitions. Honor one another's successes and life milestones, and place a high value on forming a relationship that fosters personal development and fulfillment for both parties.

In terms of roles and obligations within our marriage, how can we prevent slipping into resentment or imbalance patterns?

Proactive communication, frequent check-ins, and a readiness to address problems as they emerge are necessary to prevent patterns of resentment or imbalance. Keep an eye out for indications of imbalance or discontent in the relationship and start a conversation about constructive ways to resolve these problems. Develop empathy and understanding for one another's viewpoints, and work together to identify solutions that advance equality, justice, and marital pleasure.

To prevent one spouse from feeling entirely in charge of particular chores, how can we encourage shared decision-making and ownership of roles and responsibilities within our marriage?

To encourage shared decision-making and role and responsibility ownership, a culture of cooperation, mutual respect, and trust must be established inside the marriage. Treat duties and obligations as cooperative projects and include both parties in the decision-making process from the beginning. Promote candid communication, engaged engagement, and shared accountability for the results. As a team, recognize and celebrate accomplishments.

Chapter Four

Appreciating your partner for influential roles performed

How important is flexibility in a marriage when it comes to assigning and receiving obligations, particularly when things change over time?

Managing duties and responsibilities in a marriage requires flexibility, particularly when circumstances change over time. Be open to making necessary adjustments to fit in with new difficulties, priorities, and life stages. Openly discuss any changes in wants or expectations, and work together to come up with original solutions that promote the pleasure and well-being of both parties.

Regarding assigning and receiving tasks and obligations in our marriage, how can we cultivate a spirit of cooperation and teamwork?

Encourage cooperation and teamwork by placing a high value on honest communication, support from one n another, and a shared dedication to the marriage's success. View assignments and obligations as chances to collaborate with others to achieve shared objectives and recognize successes as a group. Establish a welcoming and inclusive atmosphere where both partners are empowered to contribute to the partnership and feel appreciated and respected.

What steps should we take if one spouse believes their contributions to the marriage are not appreciated or acknowledged?

It's critical to handle the situation with compassion and understanding if one partner believes that their contributions are not appreciated or acknowledged. It is essential to recognize and affirm their frustrations and dissatisfactions by listening to them without passing judgment. Collaborate to determine strategies for enhancing mutual respect, communication, and recognition of each other's contributions to the marriage.

In the framework of their duties and obligations in marriage, how can we make sure that both partners have

opportunities for personal development, fulfillment, and self-care?

By placing a high priority on balance and welfare in the marriage, you can make sure that both spouses have possibilities for personal development, fulfillment, and self-care. In addition to supporting one another in finding time for self-care and relaxation, encourage one another to pursue interests, hobbies, and goals outside of their positions and duties. Establish a relationship that appreciates and promotes cooperation and mutual support in addition to personal development and satisfaction.

In managing roles and obligations within our marriage, how can we strike a good balance between independence and interdependence?

Encouraging a strong sense of partnership and mutual support while also acknowledging and respecting each partner's autonomy and individuality is necessary to maintain a healthy balance between independence and interdependence. Give each other room to follow your passions and objectives, but also place a high value on cooperation, communication, and joint decision-making in all facets of your shared life. Aim to establish a partnership where the partners are profoundly attached to and dependant upon one another and where each feels free to be who they indeed are.

How can we effectively show our thankfulness and appreciation for one other's contributions, and what function do these emotions play in managing duties and responsibilities within a marriage?

Showing gratitude and appreciation is crucial to creating a happy and encouraging dynamic in a marriage, particularly when it comes to delegating and roleplaying. Regularly take the time to recognize and thank each other for the contributions that you have made, whether it is through vocal compliments, deeds of kindness, or tiny tokens of appreciation. Establish a culture of gratitude in your partnership by striving to acknowledge and commemorate each other's accomplishments daily.

How can we turn obstacles and disagreements about duties and tasks into chances for relationship-building and personal development?

When handled with tolerance, understanding, and a readiness to grow and adjust, difficulties and disagreements about roles and responsibilities can be great chances for relationship strengthening and personal development. Make use of these times to improve your understanding of one another's viewpoints, your ability to communicate and solve difficulties, and your will to stand by one another through the good times and the bad in married life.

What tools or networks of support are available to assist us in navigating our marriage's roles and responsibilities, particularly in uncertain or transitional times?

Books, workshops, counseling services, online groups, and other resources are just a few of the various tools and support networks that are available to assist couples in navigating roles and duties within their marriage. Look for resources that align with your interests and values as a couple, and don't be afraid to ask for help or advice when you need it. Keep in mind that you are not the only one in your marriage to experience difficulties and that there are many resources and techniques to assist you in overcoming them.

How can we make sure that the way we assign duties and obligations to each other changes over time to take into account changes in our situations and the dynamics of our relationships?

It takes constant communication, introspection, and adaptability to make sure that your roles and duties change and adjust as time goes on. Communicate with each other regularly to evaluate how effectively the current arrangements are functioning and to talk about any potential modifications or revisions. As circumstances and objectives change, be willing to renegotiate roles and duties. Approach the process with a shared commitment to the success of your relationship.

How can empathy for one another's experiences and viewpoints be developed, and what part does empathy play in assigning duties and obligations within a marriage?

In a marriage, empathy plays a critical role in promoting mutual support, understanding, and connection, particularly when it comes to assigning and receiving duties. Develop empathy by paying attention to each other's viewpoints and experiences, as well as by trying to comprehend the feelings and intentions that underlie each other's behavior. Put yourself in your spouse's position, think about things from their perspective, and address disagreements or difficulties with empathy and understanding.

How can we make sure that, instead of perpetuating power dynamics or traditional gender stereotypes, our allocation of tasks and responsibilities fosters equality and cooperation within our marriage?

It is essential to question established gender norms and power structures in relationships to make sure that your allocation of duties and responsibilities fosters equality and cooperation. Treat assignments and duties as team projects; do not impose expectations or value judgments based on conventional gender standards. Establish equitable authority for decision-making and responsibility ownership, and place a high value on cooperation, communication, and respect for one another in all facets of your relationship.

If one partner believes they are not carrying out their duties or obligations in the marriage, how can we deal with emotions of guilt or inadequacy that may surface?

To deal with guilt or inadequacy feelings, a relationship needs compassion, introspection, and open communication. Without passing judgment, accept and affirm each other's emotions. Then, collaborate to find workable solutions and networks of support that might lessen these emotions. Remember that no one is perfect, and try to be understanding and self-compassionate. What matters is that you both want to support each other and grow your relationship.

How many duties and responsibilities can be managed when both partners have complex jobs or outside obligations?

Effective time management, communication, and flexibility are necessary for managing duties and responsibilities when both spouses have demanding employment or outside commitments. Make it a priority to communicate openly about needs, schedules, and priorities. Work together to create solutions that balance each partner's personal and professional obligations. Assign duties, divide up domestic chores, and encourage one another to achieve contentment and balance in all facets of life.

How can we make sure that the way we assign jobs and duties is both flexible and long-lasting as things change?

Consistent communication, introspection, and necessary adjustment are necessary to make sure your roles and duties are sustainable and flexible. Periodically check in with each other to see how things are doing and talk about any modifications or adjustments that might be needed. As circumstances and objectives change, be willing to renegotiate roles and duties. Approach the process with adaptability, inventiveness, and a shared commitment to the success of your relationship.

Chapter Five

How does technology affect communication in a marriage, and how

can we make sure it strengthens rather than weakens our bond?

Why is it crucial for the general health and well-being of our marriage that we foster a sense of cooperation and partnership in handling tasks and obligations within it?

To foster a sense of cooperation and partnership, you should place a high value on communication, support from one another, and joint decision-making in every area of your marriage. View assignments and obligations as chances to collaborate with others to achieve shared objectives and recognize successes as a group.

As we go into new life stages, like becoming parents or taking care of aged parents, how do we manage changes in roles and responsibilities?

It takes open communication, adaptability, and flexibility to handle changes in roles and responsibilities. As you move through different phases of life, be prepared for and talk about any changes in your responsibilities. Work together to develop plans and tactics that can adapt to your changing priorities and requirements. As circumstances change, be ready to renegotiate roles and duties. Additionally, be patient and understanding with one another during transitions.

How can we utilize our common objectives and aspirations to direct how our tasks and responsibilities are divided in our marriage, and why is this crucial for creating a feeling of cohesion and direction?

Shared goals and aspirations should guide the division of roles and responsibilities to foster a sense of unity, purpose, and mutual investment in the marriage. Work together to determine your relationship's shared values, priorities, and long-term objectives. Then, utilize this framework to decide how to divide up duties and obligations. As you collaborate to achieve similar goals, it might be beneficial to match your division of labor with your shared vision for the future to promote a sense of motivation, fulfillment, and teamwork.

Why is it crucial to preserve a happy and healthy relationship for both parties to have chances for personal development and fulfillment while adhering to their duties and responsibilities?

It is essential to place a high value on harmony, adaptability, and mutual support in a relationship to guarantee that both parties have chances for personal development and fulfillment. Create time for self-care and personal growth, and support one another in pursuing your interests, hobbies, and objectives away from your shared obligations. Acknowledge and honor one another's successes and life milestones, and place a high value on establishing a relationship that fosters personal development and fulfillment for both partners separately and together.

When it comes to assigning roles and obligations within our marriage, how can we strike a balance between the need for spontaneity and flexibility and the requirement for structure and routine?

Discovering a middle ground that assists both parties takes open communication, compromise, and a willingness to juggle spontaneity and flexibility with structure and routine. Provide a basic structure or schedule for handling duties and responsibilities, but leave room for flexibility and modification when necessary. When it comes to carrying out your joint responsibilities, be flexible and creative. When dealing with unforeseen obstacles or adjustments, put communication and teamwork first.

How does boundary setting affect the distribution of duties and obligations in a marriage, and how can we set and uphold appropriate limits with one another?

Setting boundaries is essential to preserving respect, self-reliance, and individual liberty in a marriage, particularly when it comes to assigning and receiving duties. Discuss each other's needs, preferences, and boundaries openly and sincerely. You should also clearly define expectations and agreements for how you will handle your shared obligations. To make sure that both parties feel supported and appreciated in the relationship, respect each other's limits, and be honest when necessary about any changes or renegotiations.

Rather than having one partner feel entirely in charge of particular duties or decisions, how can we encourage a sense of cooperation and shared ownership when it comes to managing roles and responsibilities within our marriage?

It is essential to place a high value on open communication, respect for one another, and a readiness to cooperate to promote a sense of shared ownership and collaboration. Treat duties and obligations as cooperative projects and include both parties in the decision-making process from the beginning. Celebrate successes as a team and push each other to take the initiative and provide suggestions. You can improve your relationship and give your marriage cohesion and direction by encouraging a culture of cooperation and shared accountability.

How can we foster a culture in our marriage where we recognize and value each other's accomplishments, and why is this crucial to preserving a supportive and upbeat dynamic?

Prioritizing thanksgiving, validation, and acknowledgment of each other's work and achievements within the marriage is essential to fostering a culture of appreciation and acknowledgment. Spend time routinely praising and thanking each other for the contributions that you have made, whether it be through tiny gestures, vocal affirmations, or deeds of kindness. Make an effort to recognize each other's accomplishments regularly and foster an attitude of giving and acknowledgment in your relationship. You may create a helpful and upbeat dynamic in your marriage and fortify your relationship by cultivating an appreciation culture.

How do we handle changes in family dynamics, like the advent of children or taking care of aging parents, or role shifts, such as when one partner takes on a new profession or career path?

It takes open communication, adaptability, and flexibility to manage role changes. Recognize and talk about any changes in roles and duties that may come with these changes, and work together to come up with solutions that satisfy everyone's preferences and needs. As situations change, be ready to reevaluate and modify your labor allocation. Additionally, give top priority to providing compassionate and understanding support to one another during these shifts.

Regardless of conventional gender roles or cultural expectations, what measures can we take to guarantee that both partners feel empowered to assume leadership positions and make decisions inside the marriage?

The fact that both partners are capable of assuming leadership positions and making choices, it is imperative to question conventional gender roles and cultivate an environment of equality and reciprocal regard inside the marriage. Create possibilities for collaborative leadership and decision-making by supporting one another's initiative and ideas. Honor each other's accomplishments and strengths, and place a high priority on establishing a partnership in which each partner feels respected, appreciated, and empowered to make contributions to the relationship's success.

What should we do when one partner feels overburdened by their obligations and the other wants to support them but doesn't know how to go about it?

Empathy, communication, and a desire to function as a team are necessary for managing circumstances in which one partner feels overburdened. Without passing judgment, pay attention to each other's worries and emotions, and reassure each other that you are there to support one another. Work together to find workable solutions and systems of support that can lessen the load, and be willing to change roles and responsibilities to give the assistance and care that is required when needed.

How can we, as spouses with hectic schedules and conflicting expectations, prioritize activities and obligations within our marriage to foster successful time management?

Encouraging efficient time management calls for routines, priority-setting, and honest communication about obligations and schedules. Work together to draft a joint calendar or plan that lists duties and due dates, and talk about time management techniques that work for both of you. To make sure that the requirements of both partners are satisfied, be realistic about what you can achieve in the time allotted and be prepared to reevaluate and rearrange your priorities as necessary.

If one spouse believes they are carrying a disproportionate amount of marital responsibilities, how can we avoid animosity from escalating over time?

Proactive communication, frequent check-ins, and a dedication to resolving problems as they emerge are necessary to prevent resentment. Discuss each partner's thoughts and worries about the labor division openly and sincerely. Then, work together to

47

come up with solutions that advance equality and justice in the partnership. To guarantee that both partners feel appreciated, respected, and supported in their duties and responsibilities, be prepared to make changes and concessions as necessary.

In our marriage, how can we foster a culture of accountability and followthrough where both spouses accept responsibility for their actions and contributions?

Establishing a culture of accountability entails being transparent in communication, holding one another accountable for your promises, and holding each other responsible for your contributions to the marriage. Set mutually agreed upon objectives and duties, and stay in constant communication to evaluate each other's progress and resolve any problems or roadblocks. As you strive toward your shared goals, support and encourage one another while you celebrate accomplishments together.

How can we foster a flexible and adaptable mindset? What part does flexibility play in managing duties and obligations within a marriage?

Managing roles and obligations and negotiating the intricacies of marriage require flexibility. Develop a flexible mentality by remaining adaptable to new situations, being open to change, and taking on obstacles head-on with resiliency and ingenuity. As you go through changes and adjustments, be patient and understanding with one another. Communication and teamwork should be given top priority to come up with solutions that benefit both of you.

In light of their respective duties and responsibilities, how can we make sure that each partner has enough time for rest, relaxation, and self-care? Additionally, why is this crucial for preserving happiness and general welfare in the marriage?

It's essential to prioritize balance and well-being in a relationship to make sure that both partners have time for self-care, relaxation, and rest. Make time for one another to rest and recover, and support self-care routines that advance mental, emotional, and physical well-being. Acknowledge that taking pauses and establishing boundaries is crucial in preventing burnout, and encourage one another to prioritize self-care as a vital element of a happy and successful marriage.

Instead of slipping into patterns of rivalry or hatred, how can we foster a cooperative and team-oriented attitude when it comes to handling duties and responsibilities within our marriage?

Building a culture of respect, gratitude, and support amongst spouses is essential to promoting collaboration and teamwork. Treat duties and responsibilities as cooperative projects and concentrate on coming up with solutions that work for all parties. As you strive toward shared objectives, acknowledge and support one another's accomplishments and qualities. You can fortify your relationship and establish a constructive and encouraging dynamic in your marriage by placing a high value on cooperation and teamwork.

In the face of outside pressures or unforeseen obstacles that might affect our roles and responsibilities, how do we keep our marriage harmonious and balanced?

It takes resiliency, flexibility, and a dedication to helping one another through life's ups and downs to keep harmony and balance. When managing obstacles together, place a high value on teamwork, empathy, and communication. View obstacles as chances for development and learning. Remind yourself that you are stronger together than you are alone, and rely on one another for support and encouragement.

About the Author

ADEGBOYE S. ADURAGBEMI is a manager, business administrator, entrepreneur, and motivational speaker in Africa. ADEGBOYE has his BA from Yale University, IPMA from Adonai University, and a Masters in Business Administration (MBA) from the University of Salford, Manchester.

He was born in South Africa but is presently based in Nigeria as a motivational speaker and marriage counselor in institutions, sectors, and seminars with young and upcoming managers all over Africa.

Acknowledgments

I want to express my sincere gratitude to everyone who helped with the "FAQ on Communication in Marriage." Throughout this journey, their encouragement, insight, and support have been priceless.

I want to start by acknowledging the fact that, without God, this guide wouldn't have been possibly achieved.

And also to my spouse, who has always been motivating and supportive in making this task successful, I will always love and appreciate you.

I have many couples to appreciate who have shared their experiences, challenges, and victories with me over the years. Your openness, weakness, and tenacity have enhanced the book's pages and provided priceless insights into the difficulties of marriage communication.

My sincere gratitude goes out to my family and friends for their continuous support and encouragement during this journey. Your wise advice, tolerance, and words of support have helped me get through the complicated process of writing and releasing this book.

I sincerely thank the specialists and experts who have so kindly offered their knowledge and skills in marriage and communication. Your advice and thoughts have improved this book's quality and depth, and I appreciate your contributions.

Finally, I would like to express my profound gratitude to all of the readers of this work. As you journey through the process of communication in your marriage, I hope that the knowledge, direction, and encouragement provided within these pages will be a source of inspiration and empowerment for you.

I sincerely appreciate your help.